# LEGENDS

## TERRY O'NEILL

JONATHAN CAPE

THIRTY-TWO BEDFORD SQUARE

LONDON

# INTRODUCTION

He was just a guy sitting there with all the other passengers at London Airport, but he was immaculately dressed and looked distinguished. He was also fast asleep. I could see he was really wiped out; I guess that's why I photographed him. I'd just taken the picture when a newspaper reporter came over and asked to buy my picture of Rab Butler asleep – Rab Butler, who was Home Secretary in Harold Macmillan's government back then, in 1959. The next day the photograph appeared on the front page of the *Sunday Dispatch* and the editor offered me a part-time job doing photo reportage at the Airport. That's how I became a photographer. It was completely accidental, just like Alice falling down the rabbit hole.

I was born in the East End of London in 1938. When the war started my family moved to Middlesex. I remember spending almost every night in an air raid shelter, jammed into a tiny black space, listening to the bombs falling outside. I was painfully shy as a kid. If anyone came into the house, I hid under the table. I'd been playing the drums since I was ten and was an avid jazz fan. When I was fourteen I left school to work as a drummer, playing in small combos in and around London. My dream was to go to New York and study with the great drummers there, but at eighteen I had to go into the army. I was one of the last to go before compulsory National Service was abolished. It's funny to think that if the Beatles and Rolling Stones had had to do National Service the 'swinging' sixties might not have happened.

When I got out of the army I was still dreaming of America and I thought the best way of getting there was as an air steward. I applied to BOAC and the personnel officer told me I'd stand a better chance of becoming a steward if I took any sort of job with them, so I started working in their technical photographic unit. I went to

art school once a week, as part of the training, and I began to get interested in photo journalism. I bought myself a little camera, an Agfa Silette, and for fun I used to go into the passenger terminals and shoot picture stories. With so many people waiting around, arriving and saying goodbye, there was always something dramatic, emotional or funny going on. It was during one of these sessions that I took the photograph of Rab Butler sleeping.

At the beginning of the 1960s I started working full-time for the *Daily Sketch*, which was *the* picture paper in those days. The editor liked my approach. He wanted images which would capture the style and personality of the people who were beginning to make an impact and define the period. I got myself a pretty good 35-millimetre Canon and I studied every photographic book I could get my hands on. It was an innovation to take celebrity shots for a newspaper using 35-millimetre film but it reflected the times – every rule was being broken. The traditional way of photographing stars as prefabricated images completely disappeared in the 1960s. The new celebrities, people like the Beatles and the Stones, didn't want phoney, artificial shots; they wanted photographs of them to look spontaneous and natural. I was coming of age at the same time as they were and my success went hand in hand with theirs. I was named, along with Don McCullin and Philip Jones-Griffiths, as a photographer to watch. I went freelance and soon my work started appearing in magazines such as *Look*, *Life*, *Vogue*, *Paris Match*, *Rolling Stone* and *Stern*. My pictures had an international appeal and I was one of the most published photographers in the world in the 1960s and 1970s. Anyone I admired, I made sure I photographed. Then I began getting assignments as a special photo journalist on film sets, shooting the actors on and off the screen. Often the best photographs, like the one of Paul Newman and Lee Marvin (p.110), were taken when the actors weren't working.

A great camaraderie came out of the 1960s; friendships you made when you were young bore fruit later on. For example, I photographed Richard Burton when he was filming *Look Back in Anger* and got to know him quite well. Because of this early friendship I had the opportunity of taking some pictures of him with Elizabeth Taylor (p.65). When David Bowie made it big, she really wanted to meet him and I was in a position to get them together for the first time (pp.66-67). In the 1960s I was a sort of Boswell to the great personalities of the day. We used to hang out at the Ad Lib Club. The stars would work on their music and films all day and I would photograph them. Then in the evening we'd all have dinner together – actors, musicians, designers, photographers and models – and chat about our work. We never stopped to ask what it *meant*, we were simply having a great time. I was never in awe of the people I photographed. We'd all started out together in one of the biggest cultural and social revolutions for decades. Most people were about the same age and from the same sort of background – people from the working and lower classes were getting opportunities they'd never had before. What I enjoyed most was spotting a new talent, feeling that I had my finger on the pulse. I used to follow my instinct and I was frequently proved right. I spotted Elton John in the early 1970s, right at the beginning of his career, and stayed with him all the way (pp.30-34). Chris Evert Lloyd was another person I photographed just before her career took off (p.41).

Now, so many years later, I'm surprised by how much the mood of the 1960s and 1970s comes across in my pictures, much more than I'd realised at the time.

I'm also dismayed that so many of my pictures got lost. About a third of the negatives of the photographs in this book were either mislaid or destroyed. The picture of Rab Butler disappeared. I didn't take stock as I went along; I just got on with the job. I was never interested in making a name for myself. To me, the subject makes the photograph, not the photographer.

I'm often asked what I've learnt about the extraordinary lives of the celebrities I've met. One thing is clear – the people who succeed in show-business all lose something of themselves. Fame can be so destructive in so many ways. I've never lost my sense of the camera as a lethal weapon and the feeling that I'm an intruder. When someone trusts you enough to let you near them, I think you should regard it as a privilege. It's fair to say that most of the people in my pictures didn't like being photographed, and if there's one thing I've discovered, it's this: they're all as shy as I am, even Muhammad Ali.

1985                                          TERRY O'NEILL

5

10

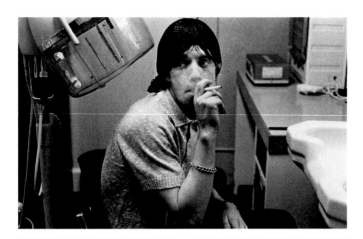

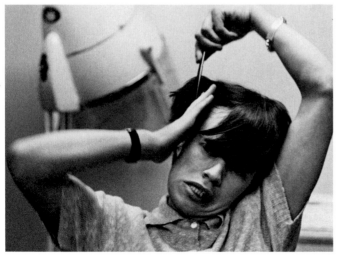

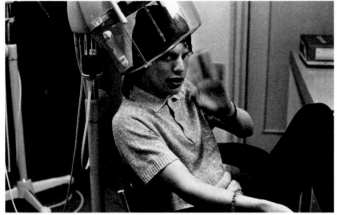

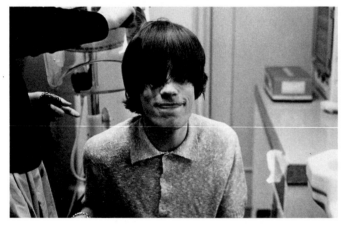

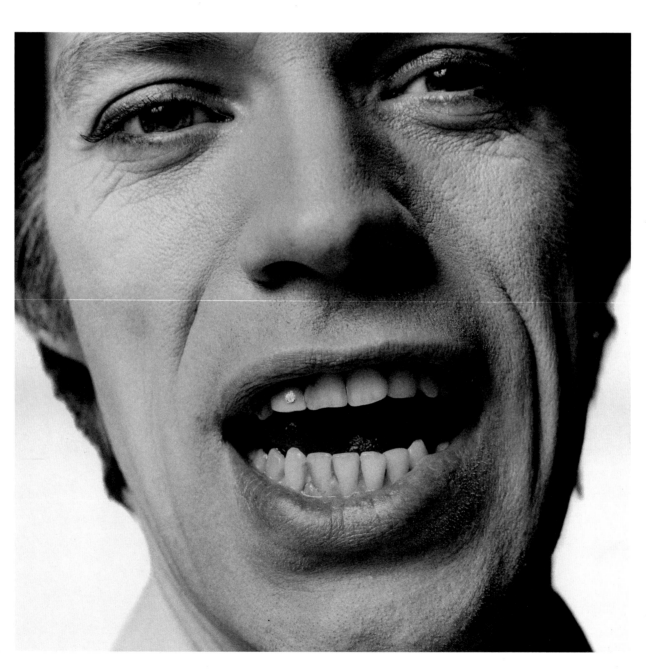

38

48

TO 121184 C

118

119

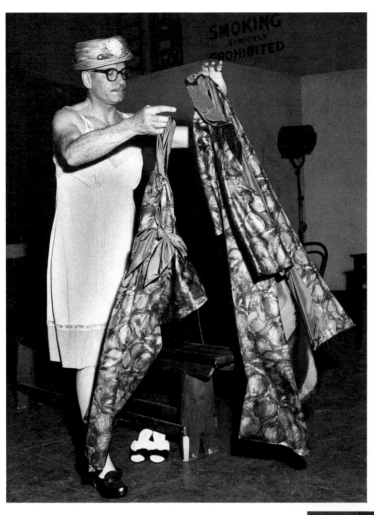

124

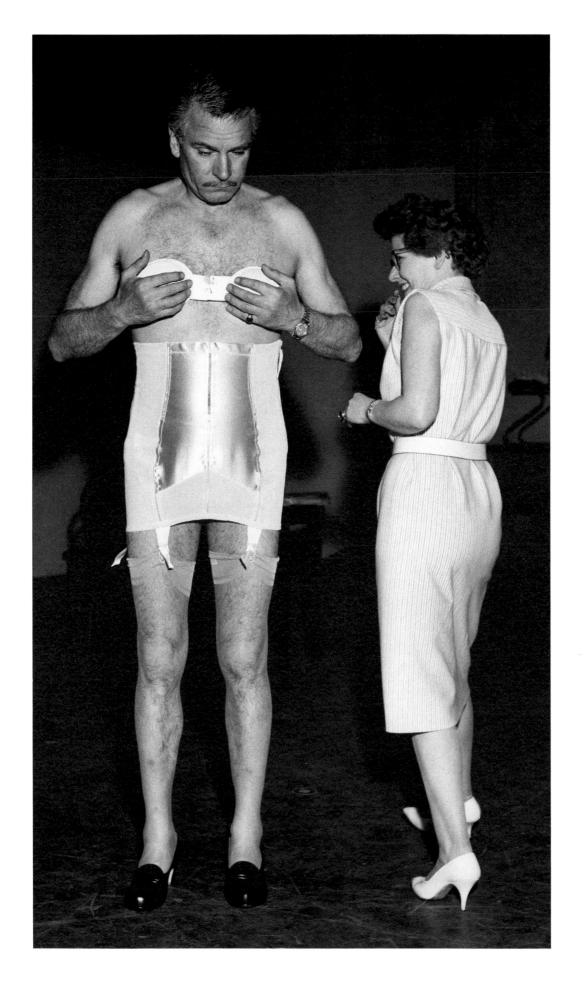

# LEGENDS

Page 6 — Frank Sinatra between takes on the set of *Lady in Cement*, Miami Beach, 1968

Page 7 — Sinatra outside his dressing-room before an engagement at the Fontainebleau Hotel in Miami Beach, 1968

Pages 8-9 — Sinatra with his stand-in (front) and his protective escorts arriving on location in Miami Beach, 1968

Pages 10-11 — Judy Garland and Liza Minnelli in London, 1962

Page 12 — Janice Joplin backstage at a Hollywood television studio, 1971

Page 13 — Sammy Davies Jr in rehearsal at the Pigalle night-club in London, 1961

Page 14 — Elvis Presley in the opening-night performance of his comeback engagement at Caesar's Palace Hotel in Las Vegas, 1970

Page 15 — Bruce Springsteen on Sunset Strip in Los Angeles to promote his album *Born to Run*, 1975

Page 16 — John Lennon in rehearsal, 1963

Page 17 — George and Olivia Harrison, Ringo Starr, Barbara Bach and her son Gianni, Paul and Linda McCartney at the wedding reception of Ringo and Barbara in London, 1982

Page 18 — Linda and Paul McCartney during a publicity session for their film *Give My Regards To Broad Street*, 1984

Page 19 — George Harrison in seclusion in Henley, England, 1975

Pages 20-21 — Rod Stewart in the grounds of his house in Old Windsor, England, 1971

Page 22 — Roger Daltrey on his estate in Sussex, England, 1978

Page 23 — Keith Moon, Roger Daltrey, Pete Townsend, and John Entwistle at Shepperton Studios, England, 1978

Page 24 — David Bowie during filming of *The Man Who Fell To Earth* in Los Angeles, 1976

Page 25 — Stevie Wonder at a children's home for the blind in London, 1970

Page 26 — Mick Jagger before a television appearance at BBC Studios, Shepherd's Bush, 1963

Page 27 — Jagger as businessman, London, 1976

Page 28 — Jagger with diamond in his tooth, London, 1976

Page 29 — Bianca Jagger in publicity for *Success*, Munich, 1978

Page 30 — Elton John at home in Beverly Hills, 1975

Pages 30-31 — Elton at Caribou Ranch, Colorado, for the recording of his album *Rock Of The Westies*, 1974

Pages 32-33 — Elton at Dodger Stadium in Los Angeles, 1975

Page 34 — Elton with waxwork Ella Fitzgerald at Madame Tussaud's, London, 1975

Page 35 — Muhammad Ali and his mother, Mrs Odessa Clay, in Dublin, 1972

Page 36 — Ali in Dublin, training for his fight with Alvin Lewis, 1972

Page 37 — Mark Spitz in London after winning seven Olympic gold medals, 1972

Page 38 — Illie Nastase and Jimmy Connors dressed for Wimbledon, 1974

Page 39 — Billie Jean King dressed as one of her idols, London, 1975

Page 40 — Billie Jean in London, 1976

Page 41 — Chris Evert during her first appearance at Wimbledon, 1972

Page 42 — Jodie Foster in London to promote the film *Bugsy Malone*, 1976

Page 43 — Tatum O'Neal in London to promote *International Velvet*, 1978

Page 44 — Princess Margaret and Lord Snowdon, 1974

Page 45 — Princess Margaret and Lord Snowdon with their children, David and Sarah, London, 1974

Page 46 — Lord Snowdon in Beverly Hills, mid-1970s

Page 47 — Peter Sellers and Lord Snowdon in Beverly Hills, mid-1970s

Page 48 — Peter Sellers as Inspector Clouseau, 1976

Page 49 — Sellers, the fanatical photographer, in Rome, 1965

Page 50 — Sean Connery on the set of *Diamonds Are Forever*, Las Vegas, 1971

Page 51 — Margaret Thatcher modelling a suit for a woman's magazine, 1976

Page 52 — Jean Shrimpton at a doll's hospital in London, 1964

Page 53 — Twiggy, London, 1975

Page 54 — Lauren Hutton, London, 1978

Page 55 — Jerry Hall posing for a lingerie feature, London, 1978

Pages 56-57 — Isabella Rossellini in publicity stills for *White Nights*, London, 1984

Page 58 — Keith Moon, London, 1975

Page 59 — Alice Cooper re-enacting a nightmare after coming out of an alcoholics' rehabilitation centre, Beverly Hills, 1979

Page 60 — Dean Martin preparing to go on stage at a Las Vegas night-club, 1971

Page 61 — Lee Marvin on set for the film *Pocket Money*, Tucson, Arizona, 1971

Page 62 — Glenda Jackson at lunch-time during the filming of *Mary Queen of Scots*, Shepperton Studios, England, 1971

Page 63 — Richard Burton playing a hairdresser in the film *Staircase*, Paris, 1969

Page 64 — Burton between takes of *The Klansman*, Oroville, California, 1974

Page 65 — Elizabeth Taylor and Burton in their trailer on location for *Villain*, Hounslow, 1971

Pages 66-67 — David Bowie and Elizabeth Taylor meeting for the first time, Beverly Hills, 1975

Page 68 — Bowie working on the album cover for *Diamond Dogs*, London, 1975

Page 69 — George C. Scott and Trish Van Devere on the set of *Beauty and the Beast*, Elstree Studios, England, 1977

Page 70 — Dudley Moore and Peter Cook relaxing in Beverly Hills, 1975

Page 71 — Jennifer Beales and Sting (as Frankenstein) in costume for the film *The Bride*, Shepperton Studios, England, 1984

Page 72 — Sean Connery and Brigitte Bardot meeting for the first time in Deauville, France, preparatory to the filming of *Shalako*, 1968

Page 73          Bardot, Spain, 1971

Pages 74-75    Marlene Dietrich taking a curtain call, London, 1975

Page 76          Ginger Rogers in her dressing-room, London, 1969

Page 77          Raquel Welch in her bedroom in Beverly Hills, 1976

Page 78          Welch in publicity still for *The Magic Christian*, London, 1970

Page 79          Monica Vitti with Peter O'Donnell (left) and Joseph Janni at Shepperton Studios during the filming of *Modesty Blaise*, 1966

Pages 80-81    Sharon Tate ten days before her death, London, 1969

Page 82          Natalie Wood, London, 1965

Page 83          Romy Schneider on vacation in St Tropez, 1972

Pages 84-85    Jane Fonda between takes during the filming of *Julia*, Norfolk, England, 1977

Page 86          Audrey Hepburn in costume for *How to Steal a Million*, Paris, 1966

Page 87          Shirley Maclaine, London, mid-1970s

Page 88          Barbra Streisand at home in Beverly Hills, 1976

Page 89          Faye Dunaway at the Beverly Hills Hotel the morning after winning an Oscar for her performance in *Network*, 1976

Page 90          Dolly Parton, London, 1977

Page 91          Mae West in publicity still for *Myra Breckinridge*, Hollywood, 1970

Page 92          Bob Hope in London for *This Is Your Life*, 1970

Page 93          Bing Crosby in a variety show, Hollywood, 1970

Page 94          Ava Gardner between takes during filming of *Mayerling*, Munich, 1968

Pages 94-95    John Huston and Ava Gardner on the set of *The Life and Times of Judge Roy Bean*, Tucson, Arizona, 1972

Page 96          George Raft at home in Beverly Hills, 1970

Page 97          Robert Mitchum, Cambridge, England, 1984

Page 98          Groucho Marx at home in Beverly Hills, 1970

Page 99          Christopher Lee (top), Vincent Price, John Carradine, and Peter Cushing in costume for *The House of Long Shadows*, Hampshire, England, 1983

Page 100        Harold Robbins on his yacht in Cannes harbour, 1975

Page 101        Jackie and Joan Collins in a London studio, 1970s

Pages 102 & 103   Joan Collins at home in London, 1970s

Page 104        Tony Curtis inspecting his make-up during the filming of *The Boston Strangler*, Hollywood, 1968

Page 105        Richard Gere, London, 1979

Page 106        Sting, London, 1983

Page 107        Steve McQueen, in his Hollywood office, 1969

Page 108        Clint Eastwood, Tucson, Arizona, 1972

Page 109        Paul Newman on the set of *The Mackintosh Man*, Pinewood Studios, England, 1973

Page 110        Newman and Marvin in costume for *Pocket Money*, Tucson, Arizona, 1972

Page 111        Newman and Eastwood in a chance meeting at a motel in Tucson, Arizona, 1972

Page 112        Former CIA director Richard Helms visiting Robert Redford during the filming of *Three Days of the Condor*, on Ryker's Island, New York City, 1975

Page 113        Anonymous, London, 1976

Pages 114-115   Albert Finney keeping fit for *Two for the Road*, at 5.30 in the morning, St Tropez, 1966

Page 116        Dustin Hoffman improvising as a vagrant, New York City's East Side, 1969

Page 117        Rudolf Nureyev on *The Muppet Show*, Elstree Studios, England, 1978

Page 118        Mikhail Baryshnikov rehearsing a scene for the film *White Nights*, Elstree Studios, England, 1984

Page 119        Natalia Makarova in a London dance studio, 1976

Page 120        Sir John Gielgud and Carol Channing in a TV special variety show at Elstree Studios, England, 1970

Page 121        Gielgud and Faye Dunaway on the set of *Wicked Lady*, Hertfordshire, England, 1983

Page 122        Lord Olivier during a break in the filming of *A Bridge Too Far*, Arnhem, Holland, 1976

Pages 123-125   To be or not to be? Olivier dressing for a variety performance in *Night of 100 Stars*, London, 1962

Page 128        John Wayne's chair on the set of *Brannigan*, London, 1975

# ACKNOWLEDGMENTS

For their friendship, understanding and encouragement:
Eve Arnold, Robert Barber, Stanly Bielecki, Allan Burry,
Woodfin Camp, Peter Campion, Mark Chivas, Dennis
Cooper, Peter Evans, Adam Faith, Leonard Franklyn, John
Friedkin, Allan Ganly, Jack Hallam, Douglas Hayward,
Leonard Hickman, Roberta Jaegar, Harold Keeble, Pat
Kingsly, Robert Levine, Patricia Newcomb, Faye and Liam
O'Neill, Kay O'Neill, Leonard, Josephine and Angela
O'Neill, Vera, Sarah and Keegan O'Neill, Caroline Pfeiffer,
John Reid, Jonas Rosenfeld, Owen Sela, Ramesh Shah, Lois
Smith, Robert Webb.

For their professional expertise: Keith Altham, Ernie
Anderson, Margaret Gardner and Warren Cowan of Rogers
and Cowan, Fred Hift, Mike Maslansky, Sheldon Roskin and
Lee Solters.

For their courtesy and co-operation: Columbia Pictures,
MGM/UA, Orion, Paramount, Twentieth Century Fox,
Warner Bros, Universal.

For my PAs, Nick Read and Madeleine Saidman; and
especially for Andrew Cowan, Tom Maschler and Ed Victor
without whom . . .

The photographs in this book were taken using the following
equipment: Canon rangefinder with 50mm and 135mm;
Leica rangefinder with 35mm, 50mm; Nikon F2 with 50mm,
85mm, 180mm; and a Hasselblad 500c with 60mm and
120mm lenses. Film stock was Kodak TRI-X and Ilford FP4.

Prints by Robin Bell, Chelsea Wharf.

Original prints of the photographs that appear in this book are
available. For further details please contact Hamiltons
Gallery, 13 Carlos Place, London W1, England.
Telephone 01-499 9493.